Witness to History

The French Revolution

Sean Connolly

Heinemann Library
Chicago, Illinois

Customer Service 888–454–2279

Visit our website at www.heinemannlibrary.com

Designed by Heinemann Library
Originated by Ambassador Litho Ltd
Printed and bound in Hong Kong, China
by South China Printing

07 06 05 04 03
10 9 8 7 6 5 4 3 2 1

Library of Congress Cataloging-in-Publication Data
Library of Congress data is on file with the Library of
Congress.
The French Revolution / Sean Connolly.
    v. cm. -- (Witness to history)
Includes bibliographical references and index.
Contents: Introduction -- Sources available -- The Old
Regime --
Election fever -- The National Assembly -- The Tennis
Court Oath -- The
king responds -- Storming the Bastille -- Order and
confusion -- The
Rights of Man -- Defining the new country -- Controlling
the king --
Calls for war -- The September Massacres -- The king is
dead -- Wars on
all fronts -- The Committee of Public Safety -- The Reign
of Terror --
The ninth Thermidor -- The Directory -- The rise of
Napoleon --
Transforming the revolution -- Legacy of the revolution --
What do we
know about the French Revolution?
  ISBN 1-40340-973-0 (HC) -- ISBN 1-4034-3637-1 (PB)
  1. France--History--Revolution, 1789-1799--Juvenile
literature. [1.
France--History--Revolution, 1789-1799.] I. Title. II.
Witness to
history (Heinemann Library (Firm))
  DC148 .C736 2003
  944.04--dc21
                              2002152090

Acknowledgments
The publishers would like to thank the following for
permission to reproduce photographs:

pp. 4, 44, 46, 50 Bridgeman Art Library; pp. 5, 13, 16, 20, 24,
26, 35, 36 Mary Evans Picture Library; p. 6 British Library;
pp. 7, 51 Lauros-Giraudon; p. 8 Robert Harding Picture
Library; p. 10 Robert Harding Picture Library (David
Martyn Hughes); p. 11 Bibliotheque Nationale; p. 12 Musee
de Beaux-Arts, Rouen; pp. 14, 18, 38, 40 Musee de la Ville
de Paris; p. 22 Fogg Art Museum, Harvard University Art
Museums; pp. 28, 43 AKG London; p. 30 Corbis (Gianni
Dagli); p. 32 Musee Carnavalet; p. 48 Hulton Getty.

Cover photograph of prisoners being taken to the
guillotine, reproduced with permission of Mary Evans
Picture Library.

The publishers would like to thank Bob Rees, historian and
teacher, for his assistance in the preparation of this book.

Every effort has been made to contact copyright holders of
any material reproduced in this book. Any omissions will
be rectified in subsequent printings if notice is given to the
publishers.

Some words are shown in bold,
like this. You can find out what
they mean by looking in the
glossary.

Contents

Introduction

You can say that the French **Revolution** changed the course of history. Many of us come across it in our everyday lives without even knowing it. We have heard of the **guillotine,** the machine for beheading people, but we might not know that thousands of French people cheered each time the blade dropped on a victim's neck. We know that July 14 is the French national holiday, but how many of us know that it marks the fall of the hated Bastille prison, where French kings used to lock up their enemies?

The French were not the first people to change the way they were governed. Nearly 100 years before the French Revolution began in 1789, Great Britain's Glorious Revolution set limits on the king's power in order to protect the public. In 1776, American **colonists** staged a revolution to gain independence from Great Britain.

Tied to tradition

The French Revolution had a flavor all its own—with the people of France rising up to rid the country of an ancient and unjust ruling system. In the late 18th century, the country was held back by a system of laws that benefited only a small group of French people. Most French people had very little say in how the country was run, although they paid enormous taxes and worked long hours. By the 1780s, it became clear that the king, along with the nobles and **clergy,** was struggling to make this outdated system work. The French people responded by rushing into a search for a better system of government.

Louis XVI ruled France when the French Revolution started. He was beheaded in 1793.

4

The ordinary people of France worked hard to scrape out a living. They soon began to realize that the government cared little for their welfare.

No turning back

The fall of the hated Bastille prison in July 1789 was the most visible early sign of the French Revolution. Elected members of the National Assembly in France struggled to write a new **constitution,** in order to right the wrongs that had triggered unrest. During these years, there was always the danger that the Revolution would be stopped dead in its tracks—either by crowds of people rioting and getting out of control, or by the foreign supporters of King Louis XVI. The French people and their new rulers had to face hard choices as the Revolution progressed.

It soon became clear that there was no place for a king in the new France of the early 1790s. **Radicals** argued that the gains of the French Revolution would only be kept by executing the king. Louis XVI was beheaded in 1793. Before long, thousands more French men and women would lose their heads. Nonetheless, despite almost constant violence during this period, the Revolution succeeded in building a richer, stronger, and fairer France.

5

How Do We Know?

By studying history we learn about the events of the past. If, for example, we need to find out about the Fall of the Roman Empire or about the Norman Invasion of England, we can find many books, articles, and other material about these subjects. They can tell us when and how these events took place, as well as who were the leading characters. They often will explain why things have happened by giving background information about the events. They also describe how the events themselves changed the course of history.

These histories are often written many years—sometimes many centuries—after the events they describe. Like any story that is told over and over, some changes can creep into the accounts. Perhaps the historian does not like French people, or Romans, or military leaders. Such a mind-set can affect how a story is told because the historian may present the facts as he or she would have liked them to occur. This kind of personal opinion is called **bias,** and it can make some historical accounts unreliable.

Of course, a historian might not be biased, but he or she may still rely on other accounts that also were written long after the original events. Such accounts are called **secondary sources** because the historian arrives at them secondhand. Here again, we must look carefully at what we are reading. The second historian might be repeating the bias or even mistakes of the previous historians.

The Reading Room at the British Museum has one of the world's greatest collections of historical sources.

Getting to the source

This book uses **primary sources** to tell the story of the French **Revolution.** These are the firsthand accounts of events. Many of the leading figures of the French Revolution were excellent writers and left a wide range of documents that reveal what they were thinking at important times. Others were skillful **orators,** and sometimes we have been able to find a written record of a speech from that time. However, the thoughts and words of ordinary French people are hard to find in written form. There are two reasons for this. First, most ordinary people were too poor to have their words published. The second reason is more important. Many of the key players—the rioting crowds, the people who captured the Bastille (see pages 18–19), and those watching the king lose his head (see pages 32–33)—were unable to read or write.

Making up our minds

Of course, primary sources can be biased as well—even those you will find in this book. Personal diaries and accounts tell the truth, but this truth is based only on what the writer knows and experiences. The letter written by Marie Antoinette (see page 9) and the account of the fall of the Bastille (see page 19) were written by people who could not—or would not—understand the full picture of what was going on around them. Other accounts were meant to urge French people to victory. Danton's stirring call to arms (see page 35) and *The Times'* report of the "September massacres" (see page 31) are examples of such **propaganda.** By recognizing the shortcomings of such primary sources, we can use them wisely to piece together the complicated jigsaw puzzle that is the French Revolution.

Our knowledge of Marie Antoinette, wife of King Louis XVI, comes from a mixture of historical accounts and her own writings.

The Old System

At the end of the 18th century, France had a system of government that was old-fashioned and, in many ways, deeply unfair. The people were divided into three groups, or "estates." The First Estate (the **clergy)** and the Second Estate (the nobles) enjoyed many privileges. Between them, they owned most of the best land in France. The Third Estate (mainly peasants and poor city dwellers, but also what we would now call the "middle class") was the largest group, but it had the least power. Representatives of these three groups were supposed to meet in the Estates-General, a type of senate. The system favored the first two estates, which could vote down almost any proposal made by the Third Estate. Moreover, the king had to summon the Estates-General, and that had not happened since 1614.

King Louis XVI had ruled France since 1774. When he came to the throne, he increased taxes to raise more money. The Third Estate was hit hardest. The king, as usual, did not want to anger the nobles by reducing their income. By the late 1780s, the French people were growing impatient for change. They also were shocked by the way Louis and his wife, Marie Antoinette, spent large sums of money on banquets, balls, and entertainment. For their part, the royal couple were unaware of the daily lives of the ordinary people. They believed that the cheers and applause that greeted them were heartfelt.

Large and beautiful mansions, such as this one at Blois, were owned by members of the First Estate—a small group of privileged people.

In 1770, Marie Antoinette, daughter of Empress Maria Theresa of Austria, became the wife of the **dauphin,** who was later crowned King Louis XVI. The following extract, taken from a letter to her mother, shows how shielded she was from life in France.

Versailles, June 14

My dearest mother,

... On Tuesday I had a fête [party] that I shall never forget all my life. We made our entrance into Paris. As for honors, we received all that we could possibly imagine; but they, though very good in their way, were not what touched me most. What was really moving was the tenderness and earnestness [seriousness] of the poor people, who, in spite of the taxes with which they are overwhelmed, were so very happy to see us. When we went to walk in the Tuileries, the crowd was so large that it was three-quarters of an hour before we could move either forward or backward. The dauphin and I gave repeated orders to the guards not to beat anyone, which had a very good effect. Such excellent order was kept during the whole day that, in spite of the enormous crowd which followed us everywhere, not a person was hurt.

When we returned from our walk, we went up to an open terrace and stayed there half an hour. I cannot describe to you, my dear mama, the joy and affection that everyone exhibited towards us. Before we left, we kissed our hands to the people, which gave them great pleasure. What a happy thing indeed it is for persons in our rank to gain the love of a whole nation so cheaply.

Election Fever

During his first fourteen years as king, Louis XVI had not been able to improve conditions in France. The country had enormous debt. Heavy taxes crippled most poor people, and industry lagged behind that of France's old rival, Great Britain. The new ideas of the period known as the **Enlightenment** were leading to calls for more justice and fairness in everyday life.

In 1788, Louis XVI called for elections to the Estates-General. Unlike today, where nearly all adults are able to vote in most countries, 18th-century France had strict limits on who could vote. Only land-owning men had the right to vote, although many of those who did qualify (including doctors, lawyers, and other educated men) were in the Third Estate, like the ordinary village and town folk. They welcomed the chance to influence the future of their country, and the election campaigns were lively. The king suspended **censorship** laws, which led to a flow of **pamphlets** calling for all sorts of changes. By the time the Estates-General met in Versailles, a town south of Paris, in May 1789, the representatives of the Third Estate had many firm proposals—and they were in no mood to be ignored.

In the seventeenth century, Louis XIV had the vast Palace of Versailles built to serve as his royal residence.

Complaints and suggestions

The following articles are taken from some of the many *cahiers* (French for "notebooks") that listed the people's complaints and suggestions for improved living conditions. The articles here seem sensible and fair, but in 1789 they were considered **radical.**

Art. 3.   French citizens should regard as laws of the
            kingdom only those that have been prepared by the
            National Assembly and approved by the king.

Art. 10.   Representatives of the Third Estate should behave in
            the same way as the representatives of the First
            and Second Estates when they address the king.

Art. 17.   All distinctions in punishments shall be abolished
            [ended]. Crimes committed by citizens of the
            different Estates shall be punished under the same
            law and in the same manner.

Art. 21.   No tax shall be legal unless accepted by the
            representatives of the people and approved by the
            king.

Art. 22.   Because all French citizens receive the same benefit
            from the government, and are equally interested in
            its maintenance, they should be taxed equally.

Art. 46.   Members of all Estates should be able to take up
            any type of work without exception [leaving any out].

Art. 64.   Judges of all law courts shall be forced to keep to
            the letter of the law and may never change or
            interpret the law at their pleasure.

The 1788 elections caused much excitement, and pamphlets calling for change were distributed in towns and villages.

The National Assembly

People of Paris and other French cities were taking a great interest in the growing political activity in France. Booklets and newspapers called for great changes, often demanding a greater say for the Third Estate. Many people believed that the representatives at the Estates-General in Versailles had a duty to bring about these changes.

All through May 1789 and into June, those representatives argued about the number of votes each Estate should have. Those in the First and Second Estates favored the existing system, which gave an equal number of votes to each Estate, even though **clergy** and nobles made up only a tiny proportion of the country as a whole. The Third Estate (which had the most representatives) preferred a system of majority voting, which would give it the greatest say. Representatives of the first two Estates blocked this idea. Finally, on June 17, the Third Estate representatives, led by Honoré Gabriel Riqueti, Count of Mirabeau (a nobleman who had switched sides), took action and declared itself the National Assembly. The ordinary people had defied those in power—and the king himself.

Arthur Young's account
Arthur Young, an English traveler, was fascinated by the political excitement in Paris at the start of June 1789. On page 13 he describes a visit to the Palais-Royal garden, which had become a center for political debate and rumor.

When the king's messenger ordered the representatives of the Third Estate to leave, their leader, the Count of Mirabeau, said, "Go and tell your master that we are here by the will of the people and we shall not budge save at the point of a **bayonet**."

The fashionable Palais-Royal gardens in Paris became a place for speeches and political debate.

I went to the Palais-Royal to see what new things were published and to obtain a catalog of all of them. Every hour produces something new. Thirteen publications came out today, sixteen yesterday, and ninety-two last week—one can scarcely squeeze from the door to the counter. Nearly all of these publications are in favor of liberty, and are often furious with the clergy and nobles... But the coffeehouses in the Palais-Royal are even more astonishing; they are not only crowded inside, but there are expectant crowds at the doors and windows, listening with open mouths to certain **orators** who address their audiences from chairs and tables. You can hardly imagine the eagerness with which they are heard, and the thunder of applause they receive for every word they say against the present government.

13

The Tennis Court Oath

The establishment of the National Assembly by the Third Estate was a serious challenge to the king and to the old system. The National Assembly then took a further step, into an area that really mattered: money. One of its first acts was to pass a new law that gave it, and it alone, the right to decide on taxes. This was a real display of defiance towards the royal government.

After hearing about this, Louis XVI acted quickly. He banned the National Assembly from its meeting hall. But on June 20, 1789, the National Assembly responded by meeting at a Versailles tennis court. In the so-called "Tennis Court Oath," its representatives swore that the National Assembly would not **dissolve** until it had drawn up a **constitution** for France. This would guarantee many rights to French people, especially benefiting the Third Estate.

The Third Estate was growing in strength, helped by splits in the ranks of the First and Second Estates. Many lower-ranking **clergy** and a number of **liberal** nobles broke away to join forces with the National Assembly. The king, of course, feared the strength of this united body. His own position would be stronger if the people were divided—that way, they would have less power to go against him. He could see, however, that opposition was gradually mounting against him.

The National Assembly gathered at a tennis court at Versailles, where they vowed to draft a new constitution.

Emmanuel–Joseph Sieyès, a priest, could have represented the First Estate but chose to support the cause of the Third Estate. His short work, "What is the Third Estate?," published in 1789, was central to the thinking that led to the Tennis Court Oath. He argued that the Third Estate was a true reflection of the country as a whole.

The Third Estate is like a strong and robust man who has one arm still tied in chains. If we were to get rid of an unfair system that favors privileged people only, the nation would be nothing less, but something more. Therefore, what is the Third Estate? It is everything, but it is tied in chains and **oppressed**. Nothing can succeed without it. Everything would be infinitely [endlessly] better if it existed alone.

It is not enough to show that privileged people, far from being useful to the nation, are in fact bad for it. It is necessary to prove that nobility is not necessary for society. In fact, it may even be a burden on a nation, and it certainly cannot make up a nation all on its own.

What is a nation? A body of people together, living under a common law, and represented by the same legal system. The Third Estate, therefore, embraces everything that belongs to the nation; and everything that is not the Third Estate cannot be regarded as belonging to the nation. What is the Third Estate? It is the whole. It is everything.

The King Responds

The setting up of the National Assembly sent shock waves through France. Louis XVI was furious, but he also knew that his position had become weaker because many members of the royal army supported the new Assembly. It would be impossible to crush the National Assembly without risking outright revolt. However, Louis felt that he had to prove that he still led the country.

On June 23, 1789, he addressed the National Assembly. His main aim was to keep the separate rights of the First, Second, and Third Estates. To demonstrate his power, he paid for loyal foreign soldiers to go to Versailles and Paris. He also dismissed the popular (and **liberal**) minister Jacques Necker from the government. However, the Third Estate stood firm. It was obvious that the public and increasing numbers from the other two Estates were on its side. The king realized that he had to show that he accepted this change in mood, or else he might face an outright revolt. On June 27, Louis ordered all the representatives of the First and Second Estates to join the National Assembly, which then called itself the National Constituent Assembly.

The French Guard (supporting the National Assembly) opens fire on German soldiers brought in and paid for by Louis XVI.

Excerpt from the king's address

In many of the most important issues, such as debating and passing laws on taxes, Louis had to give in to the Third Estate. However, this excerpt from his address to the National Assembly shows how he wanted to keep the estates separate.

The king wants the ancient distinction [separation] between the three Estates to be kept completely, as an essential part of his kingdom. He wants the elected members of the three Estates to represent the nation. The members will discuss proposals as separate groups, and will only discuss proposals together with the approval of the king. Therefore, the king declares illegal all the decisions made by members of the Third Estate since the 17th of this month.

It is I, at present, who am doing everything for the happiness of my people. I order you, gentlemen, to separate immediately, and to go tomorrow morning to your separate meeting rooms in order to start your meetings again. I order, therefore, the grand master of ceremonies to have the rooms prepared.

Storming the Bastille

The French people were in no mood for compromise. They wanted a complete victory for the representatives of the Third Estate, and they were furious that Louis XVI had dismissed Jacques Necker and brought in foreign troops. Unrest began to sweep across Paris, and the main targets were the symbols of the king's power. Full-scale rioting began on July 12, 1789. Two days later, the crowds turned on the Bastille, a royal prison. By this time there were only a few prisoners left in the Bastille, but it was still an important symbol of the power of the king. The rioters stormed and took over the Bastille, freeing the prisoners and capturing those who had guarded it.

More than any other event, the storming of the Bastille has come to represent the dramatic start of the French **Revolution.** It remains a powerful memory among French people, and Bastille Day (July 14) is still the major national holiday in France.

The storming of the Bastille on July 14, 1789, signaled the start of the sweeping changes that would shake France.

Louis de Flue's experience

A Swiss officer named Louis de Flue was one of the foreign troops brought into Paris by Louis XVI. He was one of the defenders of the Bastille, although—as this passage shows—the soldiers were not strong enough to stop those who stormed the royal prison. Also, many of the soldiers were in no mood to fight citizens who shared their political hopes.

About three o'clock in the afternoon, a troop of armed citizens mixed with some soldiers came to attack. They entered without difficulty into the courtyard. They cut the chains holding the drawbridge, and it fell open. This operation was easily carried out because the governor had ordered his troops not to fire before having warned them to leave, which we could not do while they were still at such a distance from the fortress.

After having easily dropped the bridge, the **besiegers** easily knocked down the door with axes and entered into the courtyard, where the governor went to meet them. He asked them what they wanted, and the general cry went out to "Lower the bridges!" The governor responded that he could not, and he withdrew, ordering his troops to take up defensive positions. The sieging forces brought their cannons to the gates. I stationed my men to the left of the gate.

I waited for the moment when the governor [was] to carry out his threat, and I was very surprised to see him send four people to the gates to open them and to lower the bridges. The crowd entered right away and disarmed us in an instant in the castle, threw documents from the winds, and **pillaged** everything.

Confusion and Order

The storming of the Bastille and other events in July 1789 triggered a burst of violence throughout France. Rioting crowds broke into prisons, attacked well-dressed people whom they accused of being **aristocrats,** and marched through the streets making demands. Normal activities came to a standstill. Nicola Rualt, a member of an armed patrol set up to protect property, wrote, "We could not contain the people's fury... It is not the moment to reason with them."

Provisional governments were formed to maintain order, and their rule was enforced by a new group of soldiers called the National Guard. The National Guard was placed under the command of the Marquis de Lafayette, a Frenchman who was one of the heroes of the American **Revolution.** This choice of a leader was a clever one. Lafayette was an admired and respected military leader. Even though he had helped the Americans win their War of Independence, Lafayette was not comfortable with some of the **radical** political ideas that were spreading through France. He was someone who might be able to "contain the people's fury."

Another popular hero at the time was Jean-Sylvain Bailly, a distinguished scientist. He was the first President of the National Assembly, and he also became mayor of Paris on July 15, 1789. He knew that the mood in the country was violent, and that people's expectations had changed forever.

King Louis XVI was shocked by the rising tide of revolt. He withdrew the troops that he had put in place in Paris and other cities, and he recalled Jacques Necker to the government. He also made into law the decisions that had been taken by the provisional governments.

Jean-Sylvain Bailly, an astronomer, became the first mayor of Paris in 1789.

Jean-Sylvain Bailly's diary
Jean-Sylvain Bailly's diary shows his concerns about supplying
Paris with food and his fears that people might riot if bread
supplies ran out. Ordinary Parisians would no longer hesitate
to display their anger if living conditions grew worse.

August 26:

I have already demanded that attention be
focused on providing Paris with grain. I
returned to the Assembly, and I asked that
attention be given to providing the capital
with food for the early winter months when
we can only obtain it from foreign sources. I
saw that the grain bought by the government
is running out. I thought that in a
disastrous period—at the time of a good
harvest, but one that will start being
consumed two or three months earlier than
usual—it was necessary to have a stockpile of
food in reserve. This will prevent any cause
or excuse for an uprising. Such a stockpile
could only be obtained abroad. The cartloads
of flour in our convoys are not only **pillaged**
on the way by mobs, but are also pillaged
in Paris by bakers who wait for them on the
outskirts [edge of town]. Such disorder
created two serious problems. The first is
that the distribution of flour is unequal: one
baker has too much, another not enough. The
second is that the Paris market is poorly
stocked, which upsets the public.

The Rights of Man

Despite the turmoil that gripped France, the representatives of the National Assembly never lost sight of their main task. From the outset, they had promised a **constitution** that would set out the rights and responsibilities of all French people. However, drawing up a constitution, and voting on it for approval, would take time. The French nation needed to have a clear idea of what the new constitution would do.

All through August 1789, the National Constituent Assembly set about completing a preamble, or introduction, to the constitution. The preamble would contain articles, or points, that would highlight particular rights or duties of each French citizen. Known as the Declaration of the Rights of Man, the preamble was approved on August 26, 1789. It introduced the French people to the ideas that later were used as a revolutionary slogan: *Liberté, Égalité, Fraternité* ("Liberty, Equality, **Fraternity**").

Emmanuel-Joseph Sieyès was one of the political thinkers who helped draw up the Declaration of the Rights of Man.

22

Articles from the Declaration of the Rights of Man

This selection of articles from the Declaration of the Rights of Man shows how the National Constituent Assembly aimed to guarantee many of the freedoms—of religion, free speech, and justice—that are vital in any **democracy.**

Art. 1.   Men are born and remain free and equal in rights. Social distinctions [differences] may be based only upon the general good.

Art. 2.   The aim of all political association is the preservation of the natural rights of man. These rights are liberty, property, security, and resistance to **oppression.**

Art. 4.   Liberty consists in the freedom to do everything that hurts no one else. Hence, the exercise of the natural rights of each person has no limits except those that ensure for the other members of the society the enjoyment of the same rights. These limits can only be decided by law.

Art. 9.   Because all persons are believed to be innocent until proven guilty, if an arrest is necessary, all harshness is severely forbidden by law.

Art. 10. No one shall be arrested on account of his opinions, including his religious views, provided that their expression does not disturb the public order established by law.

Art. 11. The free communication of ideas and opinions is one of the most precious of the rights of man. Every citizen may, accordingly, speak, write, and print with freedom, but shall be responsible for such abuses of this freedom, as defined by law.

Defining the New Country

After nearly a year, the National Constituent Assembly finally completed work on a **constitution** for France. Using the Declaration of the Rights of Man as a starting point, the constitution spelled out exactly how laws should be passed, how representatives should be elected, how courts should operate, and how other aspects of life in France should be conducted. Many **radical** French thinkers linked the king with everything that was bad and unfair about the old system. However, most French people, at that time, still believed that they should have a king.

The powers of the nobles and the **clergy** were another matter. During 1789 and 1790, while the constitution was being drawn up, the Assembly passed a number of laws limiting the powers of the First and Second Estates. The most important of these laws, passed on June 19, 1790, got rid of **hereditary** nobility and titles. The idea of a hereditary nobility was unacceptable because it was **undemocratic,** and it was not in keeping with the notion of equality. The new laws meant that the nobles would be citizens like other French people. The king approved the first draft of the constitution on July 14, 1790, at ceremonies in Paris attended by representatives from all parts of the nation.

Many nobles, alarmed by attacks on their property and themselves, decided to leave France and settle in other European countries.

Decree of the National Constituent Assembly

The late eighteenth century in France was a time not only of revolution, but of **Enlightenment.** Many of the new laws passed by the National Constituent Assembly removed the outward signs of noble power and privilege.

Decree Abolishing Hereditary Nobility and Titles
(June 19, 1790)

Art. 1. The National Constituent Assembly decrees [declares] that hereditary nobility is forever abolished. Consequently, the titles of Prince, Duke, Count, Marquis, Viscount, Vidame, Baron, Knight, Lord, Squire, Noble, and all other similar titles shall neither be accepted by, nor granted upon, anyone at all.

Art. 2. A citizen may assume only the real name of his family. [Until then, nobles would take the name of the region they owned as their last name.]

Art. 3. The titles of Your Royal Highness and Your Royal Highnesses shall not be granted to any group or individual, nor shall the titles of Excellency, Highness, Eminence, Grace, and so on. However, no citizen can take the liberty of attacking either monuments in churches or documents concerning families or properties.

Art. 4. The present decree does not apply to foreigners.

Controlling the King

Life for Louis XVI was difficult in the first years of the French **Revolution.** His powers were limited with each new law passed by the National Constituent Assembly. Many revolutionaries feared that Louis would try to persuade foreign kings to crush the Revolution. Other European kings would welcome the chance to end the anti-royalist revolution in France, because they were afraid of it spreading to their own countries and reducing their power. As a result, Louis and his family were watched very closely by the new French government. The royal family tried to escape in June of 1791 but were captured and returned. This attempted escape turned public opinion against the king even more.

On July 17, 1791, thousands of **republicans** gathered in Paris and demanded that the king be overthrown. Republicans believed that their leaders should be elected. Troops opened fire on the republican demonstrators. The bloodshed widened the gap between the republican and **conservative** sections of the population. After suspending Louis for a brief period, the **moderate** majority of the National Constituent Assembly reinstated the king. They hoped that his continued presence would prevent foreign powers (including Great Britain) from invading on his behalf.

The bloodshed of July 17, 1791, when many protesters were shot dead, divided France even further.

Today, when his only payment for so many sacrifices consists of mainly seeing the monarchy destroyed, and total chaos taking the place of law, the king, having protested against all the laws passed during his captivity, believes it is his duty to place before Frenchmen and the entire universe an account of his behavior and that of the government that has established itself in the kingdom.

But the more sacrifices the king made for the benefit of his people, the more the rebels labored to paint the monarchy in the most false and hateful colors.

The calling of the Estates-General, the doubling of the representatives of the Third Estate, the king's efforts to eliminate all difficulties that might delay the meeting of the Estates-General, all the reductions that the king made in his personal expenses, all the sacrifices that he made for his people in the session of June 23, all his efforts, all his generosity, all his devotion to his people—all have been misjudged, all have been misrepresented.

Calls for War

Early 1792 saw French people of all political sides calling for war. Many French nobles had fled the country and sought the aid of foreign powers to crush the **Revolution.** Some of those countries, such as Great Britain and Austria, were **monarchies** and felt threatened by the spread of revolutionary ideas from France.

Within France, there were calls for war from two directions. Supporters of the king welcomed the idea of a foreign invasion that would restore the old system. **Republicans** believed such an invasion was likely, and that France needed to strike first to defend itself and to protect the gains of the Revolution.

On April 20, 1792, the **Legislative** Assembly—which, by this time, had replaced the National Constituent Assembly—declared war on the Austrian part of the **Holy Roman Empire.** This began the series of conflicts that made up the French Revolution. The public had strong feelings and believed that the Revolution was soon to be tested to the limit.

Eager to defend the revolutionary gains of recent years, French troops (in blue) marched into battle against Austria.

"La Marseillaise"

"La Marseillaise," the French national anthem, was composed on April 24, 1792, by Claude-Joseph Rouget de Lisle. Volunteer soldiers from the southern city of Marseilles sang it as they entered Paris. The words of this song (the first verse is below in both French and English) echo the strong feelings of those who vowed to defend revolutionary France.

Allons enfants de la Patrie
Le jour de gloire est arrivé.
Contre nous, de la tyrannie,
L'étandard sanglant est levé,
l'étandard sanglant est levé,
Entendez-vous, dans la campagnes.
Mugir ces farouches soldats
Ils viennent jusque dans nos bras
Egorger vos fils,
vos compagnes.

Let us go, children of the fatherland
Our day of glory has arrived.
Against us stands tyranny,
The bloody flag is raised,
The bloody flag is raised.
Do you hear in the countryside
The roar of these savage soldiers
They come right into our arms
To cut the throats of your sons,
your country.

The "September Massacres"

By the summer of 1792, France was at war with a number of European enemies known as the Allies: notably Austria, Great Britain, and Prussia. The French suffered a series of defeats, and the Allied commander (the Duke of Brunswick) threatened to destroy Paris if the royal family was mistreated. Far from moving the people to protect the royal family, this threat caused many French people to view the king as siding with the enemy. On August 10, 1792, a group of **radical** Parisians and volunteer soldiers stormed the Tuileries, the palace where the king lived, and massacred the king's Swiss guard. Louis XVI and his family fled to the nearby hall of the **Legislative** Assembly, which promptly suspended the king and placed him in **confinement.**

The radicals, led by the lawyer Georges Jacques Danton, also took over the Parisian government, and soon gained control of the Legislative Assembly. After new elections, it became the National Convention. Between September 2 and September 6, more than 1,000 supporters of the king and suspected traitors were rounded up and killed. Even supporters of the revolution were at risk, if they were judged to be not radical enough or had behaved suspiciously in the eyes of the radicals. The prisoners had mock "trials," often led by drunken troublemakers who stirred public fears about traitors helping foreign forces. These killings became known as the "September massacres."

The storming of the king's palace, the Tuileries, marked the beginning of the end for Louis XVI, and for the monarchy in France.

Article from *The Times*
The British government, along with most members of the British press, opposed the French **Revolution.** This account, from *The Times* of September 10, 1792, paints a vivid picture of the violence of the "September massacres."

The Times

September 10, 1792

The number of **clergy** found in the Carmelite Convent was about 220. They were handed out of the prison door two by two into the Rue [street] Vaugerard, where their throats were cut. Their bodies were fixed on **pikes** and exhibited to the wretched victims who were next to suffer. The mangled bodies of others are piled against the houses in the streets; and in the quarters of Paris near to which the prisons are, the carcasses lie scattered in hundreds, diffusing [spreading] **pestilence** all around.

The streets of Paris, strewed with the carcasses of the mangled victims, are become so familiar to the sight that they are passed by and trod on without any particular notice. The mob think no more of killing a fellow creature, who is not even an object of suspicion, than wanton [wild] boys would of killing a cat or a dog. We have it from a Gentleman who has been but too often an eye witness to the fact. In the massacre last week, every person who had the appearance of a gentleman, whether stranger or not, was run through the body with a pike. He was of course an **aristocrat,** and that was a sufficient crime. A ring, a watch chain, a handsome pair of buckles, a new coat, or a good pair of boots–in a word, every thing which marked the appearance of a gentleman, and which the mob fancied– was sure to cost the owner his life. EQUALITY was the pistol, and PLUNDER [robbery] the object.

The King is Dead

The National Convention, formed after the 1792 elections, represented a new, and more **radical,** phase of the French **Revolution.** Its representatives were elected through **universal suffrage,** which meant that every man had the right to vote. The Convention abolished the remaining powers of the monarchy, and declared a **Republic** for the first time. From this point onwards, the nation's leaders always would be elected. However, simply having Louis XVI overthrown still was not enough for many people, who thought he would be free to gain foreign support. These people would only be satisfied if all royalty were eliminated—and the king with it.

The Convention accused Louis of **treason.** On January 15, 1793, by an almost **unanimous** vote, the Convention found the king guilty. Shortly afterwards, by a vote of 380 to 310, the representatives approved the death penalty. It was a close margin—there still were many who did not want the king to be executed. At eight o'clock on January 21, 1793, a guard of 1,200 soldiers arrived to escort the former king on a two-hour carriage ride to his place of execution. The execution was swift, with Louis's head severed from his body with the **guillotine**—soon to become a symbol of terror and death in Paris. There was no turning back for the Revolution now.

Louis XVI faced his executioners with dignity. His beheading was a turning point in the French Revolution; France was now a Republic.

Henry Essex Edgeworth's account
Louis XVI was accompanied to his execution by a priest, Henry Essex Edgeworth, an Englishman living in France. Edgeworth recorded the event, and in this excerpt he and the king have reached the scaffold of the guillotine itself.

The path leading to the scaffold was extremely rough and difficult to pass; the King was obliged to lean on my arm, and I feared for a moment that his courage might fail. But what was my astonishment, when arrived at the last step, I felt that he suddenly let go my arm, and I saw him cross with a firm foot the breadth of the whole scaffold and in a voice so loud... I heard him pronounce distinctly [clearly] these memorable words, "I die innocent of all the crimes laid to my charge. I Pardon those who have occasioned my death. And I pray to God that the blood you are going to shed may never be visited on France."

He was proceeding when a man on horseback, in the national uniform, with a ferocious cry ordered the drums to beat. Many voices were at the same time heard encouraging the executioners. They dragged him under the axe of the guillotine, which with one stroke severed his head from his body. The youngest of the guards immediately seized the head, and showed it to the people. At first, an awful silence prevailed; at length, some cries of 'Vive [long live] la Republique!" were heard. By degrees, the voices multiplied and, in less than ten minutes, this cry, a thousand times repeated, became the universal shout of the multitude [many], and every hat was in the air.

Wars on All Fronts

The execution of Louis XVI was a milestone in the French **Revolution.** His death showed the French people—and other nations—that there was no turning back. The effect was very powerful, and many Europeans felt that revolutionary ideas would soon spread from France and lead to violence across Europe. The major European powers decided to take action and planned to attack France. By March of 1793, France saw these enemies gathering at its northern and eastern borders. An Austrian army captured Aachen (a German city controlled by the French), and another army—made up of British, Dutch, and German troops—gathered in Holland.

At about the same time, a new threat to the Revolution developed inside the borders of France. **Royalists** and religious leaders stirred up the population of the Vendée, a region in western France, into outright revolt against the Revolutionary government. They called for a return to royal rule and for the rights of the Catholic Church to be restored.

The National Convention ordered 300,000 new **conscripts** to defend France against outside invaders—and to defend the Revolution against its enemies within France itself. Would they be enough?

Georges Jacques Danton, who had swept to the main stage of power during the "September massacres" (see pages 30–31), was now at the heart of the problems facing France. He was a powerful speaker and political leader, who could influence people's opinions with a carefully chosen phrase. As a government leader, he also needed to judge France's real position in the outside world. So in early March of 1793 he went on a secret mission to Belgium to judge the threat. He returned on March 10 to find Paris in a state of near panic. Danton realized that the new French government faced a deadly threat, but he also knew that France was sure to lose if the people continued to panic.

Danton's speech
Danton gave many stirring calls to arms in defense of the French Revolution. In the following passage of his speech to the National Convention, he relies on his own reputation for violence to urge French citizens to follow his example.

See, citizens, the fair destinies that await you. What? You have a whole nation as a lever and you have not yet upturned the whole world! To do this we need firmness and character, and to tell the truth, we lack it. I put to one side all passions. They are all strangers to me apart from the passion I have for the public good.

When the enemy was at the gates of Paris, I said to those in charge, 'Your discussions are shameful. I can see only the enemy. [Applause from the Convention.] You tire me by your squabbling, instead of occupying yourselves with the safety of the republic. You are all traitors to our country!" I said to them, 'What do I care for my reputation? Let France be free, even though my name is cursed!" What do I care that I am called a 'blood-drinker'? Well, let us drink the blood of the enemies of humanity, if need be, but let us struggle—let us achieve freedom.

Georges Jacques Danton was a lawyer and fiery **orator**, who urged his fellow citizens to fight for France.

35

The Committee of Public Safety

France listened to Danton's words and prepared to face its foreign enemies. But the home front was divided between **radicals,** who favored immediate sweeping changes, and the more cautious **moderates.** Their disputes in the National Convention weakened France's ability to make quick decisions. As a result, on April 6, 1793, the Convention established the nine-member (later changed to twelve-member) Committee of Public Safety, as the main governing body of the **Republic.** This move marked the beginning of another, yet even more radical, phase of the **Revolution:** hard-liners had control of the new ruling group.

The Committee of Public Safety helped bring calm to the economy, and it began to form a national army. One of its main aims was to deal with French antirevolutionary groups, mainly in the south and west. It set up revolutionary **tribunals** to deal with suspected traitors. Many of the accused actually supported the Revolution—but not enough, in the eyes of the radicals. Crowds filled the rooms for some trials, as famous people awaited their fate. Those who were convicted faced the **guillotine.**

The guillotine was invented by Joseph Guillotin. Its purpose was to quickly and efficiently execute the many French citizens thought to be enemies of the Revolution.

J.G. Millingen's account
In October of 1793, English citizen J.G. Millingen witnessed the trial of more than a dozen suspected **counterrevolutionaries** at the Paris Revolutionary Tribunal. Here he describes the progress of the condemned on the way to their execution.

The process of execution was also a sad and heart-rending spectacle. In the middle of the Place de la Revolution [a large space in central Paris, now known as the Place de la Concorde, or 'Peace Square'] was erected a guillotine, in front of a colossal [huge] statue of Liberty, represented seated on a rock, a Phrygian cap [a floppy cap that revolutionaries used as a symbol of liberty] on her head, a spear in her hand, the other reposing [resting] on a shield. On one side of the **scaffold** were a sufficient [large enough] number of carts with large baskets painted red to receive the heads and bodies of the victims.

Those carrying the condemned moved on slowly to the foot of the guillotine. The culprits were led out in turn, and, if necessary, supported by two of the executioner's attendants... but their assistance was rarely required. Most of these unfortunates ascended the scaffold with a determined step—many of them looked up firmly on the mincing [chopping] instrument of death [the guillotine], beholding for the last time the rays of the glorious sun, beaming on the polished axe.

The Reign of Terror

As 1793 became 1794, the Committee of Public Safety and its revolutionary **tribunals** stepped up the hunt for those who they believed threatened the **Revolution.** Maximilien Robespierre became the dominant member of the Committee. Robespierre was single-minded about protecting the gains of the Revolution. He was pitiless towards those he regarded as enemies. It seemed that he would stop at nothing—even mass executions—to achieve his aim.

No one was safe in what came to be known as "the Reign of Terror." **Moderates** who opposed the execution of Louis XVI were branded as traitors. Among them was the Marquis de Lafayette, who had supported the American Revolution and played a public role in French events after 1789. When he was denounced as a traitor, he gave himself up to the Austrian army that was poised to attack France. On October 16, 1793, Queen Marie Antoinette was executed, and 21 leading moderates were beheaded on October 31. This began a deadly wave of trials and executions lasting more than a year. Revolutionary tribunals were responsible for the execution of almost 17,000 French citizens. The victims of the Reign of Terror totaled approximately 40,000, including those who died in overcrowded, disease-ridden prisons, and rebels executed on the field of battle.

Marie Antoinette was judged by the Revolutionary Tribunal Court in October 1793, before being sentenced to death like her husband Louis XVI.

The writings of Robespierre

Robespierre knew that many people accused him of leading a **despotic** government. As this excerpt from early 1794 reveals, he believed that terror was an acceptable weapon in the battle to preserve the French Revolution.

It has been said that terror is the basis of despotic government. Does your government, therefore, resemble despotism? Yes, just as the sword that gleams in the hands of the heroes of liberty resembles that with which the supporters of **tyranny** are armed. Let the despot govern by terror his brutalized subjects; he is right, as a despot. Subdue by terror the enemies of liberty, and you will be right, as founders of the **Republic.** The government of the revolution is liberty's despotism against tyranny. Is force made only to protect crime? And is the thunderbolt not destined to strike the heads of the proud? "Indulgence for the royalists," cry certain men, "Mercy for the villains!" No, mercy for the innocent, mercy for the weak, mercy for the unfortunate, mercy for humanity.

Society owes protection only to peaceable citizens. The only citizens in the Republic are the **republicans.** For the Republic, the **royalists,** the **conspirators,** are only strangers or, rather, enemies. This terrible war waged by liberty against tyranny—is it not indivisible? Are the enemies within not the allies of the enemies without?

The Fall of Robespierre

Under the leadership of Robespierre, the government introduced many changes to France. The Catholic Church and other organized religions lost even more power and property. Even the calendar was changed. The year 1793 became known as Year I, because that is when the **Republic** was declared. (The year actually began on September 22, 1792, and ended on September 21, 1793.) New names of months reflected things in nature rather than ancient gods.

At the same time as all of these social changes, the Reign of Terror continued. By mid-1794, French **revolutionary** forces began to achieve a number of military successes. Some people began to question Robespierre's leadership, wondering whether all the violence was still necessary. Louis Freron, in his newspaper *L'Orateur du Peuple [Voice of the People]*, began accusing Robespierre of being a **dictator.** Many others echoed this view. Robespierre's time ran out suddenly on July 27, 1794, when the National Convention voted to arrest Robespierre. He and 98 of his followers were seized and beheaded the next day.

Robespierre and his followers were seized and arrested on July 29 (known in the new calendar as "the Ninth Thermidor"). They were executed the following day.

Pierre-Toussaint Durand de Maillane's account

Pierre-Toussaint Durand de Maillane, a **moderate** representative, describes what happened in the Convention Hall on July 27, 1794. Robespierre faced an organized attack by other members of the Committee of Public Safety and was condemned by the National Convention.

Meanwhile, the Reign of Terror was reaching its end. Robespierre had become unbearable, even to his own supporters. The members of the committees were in a power struggle with him, and were afraid that, sooner or later, they would become his victims. When faced with his **tyranny** in the convention, everyone whimpered, not daring to attack him. Several of those who had been threatened could no longer sleep, so, to defend themselves, they plotted against Robespierre. But how to go about overthrowing him? Robespierre was in charge of all of the Parisian authorities and counted Henriot, the commander of the armed forces, among his devoted followers. Only a ruling from the convention could fell this giant.

Robespierre went up to the **rostrum**. The only words that could be heard were 'Down with the **tyrant!** Arrest him!" Robespierre turned to us and said, 'Deputies of the right, men of honor, men of virtue, let me speak, since the **assassins** will not." He hoped to receive this favor as a reward for the protection he had given us before. But our party was decided. There was no answer, just dead silence until the debate over the decision to arrest Robespierre and his supporters, for which we all voted in favor, which made the decision **unanimous.**

The Directory

By 1795, the **Revolutionary** armies had restored peace to the French borders, but, once again, turmoil threatened to sweep across France itself. The National Convention (now controlled by the **moderate** and **conservative** representatives, who had condemned Robespierre) could not prevent new outbreaks of **radical** demonstrations.

On August 22, 1795, the Convention adopted a new **constitution,** which tried to find a balance between the radical and conservative forces to maintain national unity. In a move to satisfy radicals, the new constitution granted full citizenship (and voting rights) to all men aged 21 and over. But only property owners or men in full-time work could stand for political office. The constitution also established new sources of power within France. A five-member Directory had central, or **executive,** power (like that of a modern prime minister or president). Two elected bodies had **legislative** power (like that of a parliament or congress), which meant that they could pass new laws. These were: the Council of Elders, with 250 members, and the Council of the Five Hundred.

This system seemed to work well on paper, but soon there were divisions within the government. Demonstrations and rebellions from the general public also developed. Some of these rebellions, such as that of the radical François Noël Babeuf, threatened to overthrow the government itself. Other people simply wanted to be able to live in peace and to afford their next meal—no matter what type of government ruled the country.

As well as dealing with political attacks from all fronts, the Directory had a much more serious problem—keeping France supplied with food and other essential goods. A British naval **blockade** prevented France from getting these goods from overseas, and much of the food produced within France went to the armies. The government had to restrict the sale of basic foods, candles, and firewood just as the first frosts of a severe winter froze the country at the beginning of November 1795. Some of these goods were available at hugely increased prices in Paris and other cities through the **black market.** Elsewhere, people faced starvation.

This brief diary account of Parisian Celestin Guillard de Floriban captures the atmosphere in the French capital during the winter of 1795–96.

The price of everything is excessive. No more order, no more supervision—everybody free to sell what he has for whatever he wants. It really seems that the time has come at last to die of hunger and cold, lacking everything. Great God, what a **Republic!** And the worst of it is, one can't tell when or how it will end. Everybody is dying of hunger.

François Noël Babeuf was a radical who believed that the Revolution had not gone far enough. His calls for equal distribution of land and income were a great threat to the Directory.

The Rise of Napoleon

The Directory governed France for the next four years, but its rivalries and divisions continued to threaten peaceful government within France. However, France was making great progress in its activities abroad. A little-known officer from the French island of Corsica, Napoleon Bonaparte, was an outstanding military leader in France's time of need.

In 1793, Napoleon drove out a British fleet from the French port of Toulon, and in 1795 he crushed a disturbance in Paris. By 1796 he had been promoted several times, and he commanded the French army in Italy. He defeated four Austrian generals in a row and forced Austria to make peace. Napoleon's string of successes continued in the eastern Mediterranean region. In 1798, he conquered Turkish-controlled Egypt and defeated the Turks again in 1799.

Seeing Napoleon as a possible national leader, several French politicians overthrew the troubled Directory on November 9, 1799. They approved yet another **constitution** on December 24, 1799. This constitution gave power to a body called the Consulate, but real power went to the First Consul. The man chosen to be First Consul was General Napoleon Bonaparte.

Napoleon Bonaparte became a national hero after his military victories. After so many years of turmoil, France was ready for a strong leader.

Napoleon's statement

Just how Napoleon achieved power on November 9, 1799, is a matter of disagreement even today. But Napoleon knew that he needed the support of the French people. His first public statement the following day provides his version of events.

November 10, 1799

On my return to Paris, I found division among all the authorities and agreement upon only one point: that the constitution was half destroyed and could not save liberty. All parties came to me, confided to me their plans, disclosed their secrets, and asked for my support. I refused to be one party's man. The Council of Elders summoned me, and I went. An outline for general restoration had been planned by the men whom the nation has become accustomed to regarding as the defenders of liberty, equality, and property. The Council of Elders gave me control over the forces necessary to ensure its independence. I believed it my duty to accept the command, for my fellow citizens, for the soldiers being killed in our armies, and for the national glory acquired at the cost of their blood.

I appeared before the Council of Five Hundred just as I had before the Elders—alone, unarmed, my head uncovered—and was applauded. I had come to remind the majority of its will, and to assure them of their power. Deputies, armed with knives, rushed at me. At the same moment, cries of "outlaw" were raised against me, the defender of the law. It was the fierce cry of **assassins** against the power that was destined to suppress them.

Guards took the armed deputies away. The majority, freed from their attacks, returned peaceably into the meeting hall, listened to the proposals on behalf of public safety, and drafted the resolution that is to become the new law of the Republic.

Transforming the Revolution

During the rule of the Consulate, Napoleon Bonaparte carried through a series of reforms that had started during the **Revolution.** He established the Bank of France, strengthened the school system, made government jobs open to all who were qualified for them, and established a system of justice known as the Napoleonic Code. Many of the **radical, democratic** goals of the Revolution were put aside, but France was strengthened at home. France also launched a series of military campaigns, and by 1806 it controlled much of western Europe.

Napoleon became more and more powerful. He changed the **constitution** to give himself even more power than he had as First Consul. In 1802, he became First Consul for life (dismissing the Revolution's idea of elected leadership). Two years later, he had himself declared Emperor. This political situation was far removed from the ideals of the Revolution, but many French people believed that their life was better under Napoleon. Also, they felt that Napoleon had preserved many of the most important achievements of the Revolution in the areas of education, justice, and business.

The Battle of Trafalgar in 1805 was one of the major naval battles in history. The British, under Admiral Horatio Nelson, defeated the combined French and Spanish fleet and ruined Napoleon's plans to invade England.

Napoleon's measures against the British

In 1806, Napoleon announced the Continental System, a series of measures to stop British goods from reaching Europe. Britain had opposed the Revolution and had formed several alliances to stop Napoleon's progress. It had **blockaded** French-controlled territories so Napoleon decided to use the same tactic against Britain.

From our imperial camp at Berlin, November 21, 1806

Napoleon, Emperor of the French and King of Italy, in consideration of the fact:

1. That England does not recognize the system of international law universally observed by all civilized nations.

5. That England's monstrous abuse of the right of blockade has no other aim than to prevent communication among the nations and to raise the commerce and the industry of England upon the ruins of that of the continent.

7. That this policy of England, worthy of the earliest stages of barbarism [brutality], has profited that power to the **detriment** of every other nation.

We have consequently [as a result] decreed and do decree the following:

Art. I. The British Isles are declared to be in a state of blockade.

Art. II. All commerce and all correspondence with the British Isles are forbidden.

Art. III. Every individual who is an English subject, of whatever state or condition he may be, who shall be discovered in any country occupied by our troops or by those of our allies, shall be made a prisoner of war.

Art. IV. All warehouses, merchandise, or property of whatever kind belonging to a subject of England shall be regarded as a lawful prize.

Art. V. Trade in English goods is prohibited, and all goods belonging to England or coming from her factories or her colonies are declared a lawful prize.

Legacy of the Revolution

The abolition of the **monarchy** was the most direct result of the French **Revolution.** The Revolution was also responsible for destroying the **feudal** privileges of the nobles. With these major powers swept away, the Revolution transformed French society. A series of revolutionary laws ensured that wealth and property were distributed more equally within the country. With these laws in place, France became the European nation with the largest proportion of small, independent landowners. Other revolutionary reforms included abolishing imprisonment for debt, introducing the metric system, and establishing a national educational system.

The ideals of the Revolution—often expressed by the words "Liberty, Equality, and **Fraternity"**—have inspired freedom-seekers for more than two centuries. Dozens of countries have adopted versions of France's "tricolor" flag as a tribute to those who struggled for **democracy** in France from 1789 onwards.

The writer Victor Hugo was the son of a general in Napoleon's army. He grew up with a sense of pride in the achievements of the French Revolution.

While **exiled** from France for his **radical** political views, Victor Hugo wrote many of his greatest works. His writings, which include *The Hunchback of Notre Dame* and *Les Misérables,* reveal his deep sympathy for the lives of ordinary people.

Victor Hugo (1802–85) was one of France's greatest authors of the 19th century. He was a passionate **republican** and strong supporter of the French Revolution. As time passed, however, his views were considered too radical, and he was forced to go into exile (1852–70). In this excerpt, he shows the human, **democratic** achievements of the Revolution.

Out of this chaos of shadow spread immense rays of light parallel to the eternal laws—rays that have remained on the horizon, visible forever in the heaven of the peoples, and which are: one, justice; another, tolerance; another, goodness; another, right; another, truth; another, love.

The National Convention proclaimed this grand truth: "The liberty of each citizen ends where the liberty of another citizen commences," which in two lines makes up all human social law. It abolished slavery. It proclaimed civic joint responsibility. It decreed free education. It organized national education by the normal school of Paris: central schools in the chief towns, primary schools in the communes. It created the academies of music and the museums. It decreed the unity of weights and measures, and the unity of calculation by the decimal system.

Of the 11,210 decrees that came from the Convention, a third had a political aim, and two-thirds had a human aim. It declared that universal morality was the basis of society, and that universal conscience [thought] was the basis of law.

What Have We Learned from the French Revolution?

The French **Revolution** was full of **contradictions,** moving back and forth from **radical** reform to **conservative** reaction. Despite its unpredictable nature, the Revolution did have a force of its own. Certain events meant that there would be no turning back. The Third Estate, by becoming the dominant power in the National Assembly, made sure that its voice would ring loudest in years to come. By overcoming the symbolic Bastille, the revolutionaries knew that the king's power could be overturned. Louis XVI's execution in 1793 was almost unavoidable, as was the fearful antirevolutionary response of other European monarchs. It was not surprising that Robespierre and his allies would inflict the Reign of Terror in an attempt to stifle any protests against the new **Republic.**

French Revolutionary ideals also took root elsewhere. The Tree of Liberty being cut down in this painting had marked the founding of a short-lived republic in Naples, Italy, in 1799.

Later still, Napoleon's rise as a forceful figure of central power was the next step. We can look back at all of these stages and see patterns. These patterns appeared in later violent revolutions—especially in Russia and China. Since 1798, the revolutionary cries of "Liberty, Equality, and **Fraternity**" have rung out, inspiring nations and people around the world.

Alexis de Tocqueville's view
The noble Alexis de Tocqueville (1805–59) was a historian, social critic, and politician who wrote *The Old Régime and the French Revolution* (1856). In the excerpt on page 51, he describes the draw of the Revolution even after nearly seven decades.

I have always believed that the effort of making France a free nation (in the true sense of the word) was noble and bold. I find it to be bolder every day, but at the same time to be nobler, so that, if I could be reborn, I would prefer to risk myself completely in this daring adventure than to bend under the necessity of being a servant. Will others be happier than we have been? I do not know. Changes that were made in the social state, in the institutions, in the mind, and in the social customs of the French as the Revolution progressed—that is my subject. For seeing it well, I have up to now found only one way: that is to live, in some manner, each moment of the Revolution with the **contemporaries** by reading, not what has been said of them or what they said of themselves since, but what they themselves were saying then, and, as much as possible, by discovering what they were really thinking. The minor writings of the time and private correspondence are even more effective in reaching this goal than the debates of the assemblies. By the route I am taking, I am reaching the goal I am setting for myself, which is to place myself successively in the midst of the time. But the process is so slow that I often despair of it. Yet, is there any other?

Alexis de Tocqueville had lived for years in the newly independent United States. He was in a good position to compare the contributions made by the two revolutions—in America and in his homeland.

Timeline

1789	May 5: Meeting of the Estates-General
	June 17: National Assembly declared
	June 20: Tennis Court Oath
	July 14: Storming of the Bastille
	August 27: Declaration of the Rights of Man
	October 5–6: Outbreak of the Paris mob. **Liberal constitution** retains monarchy
1790	June 19: All **aristocratic, hereditary** titles are abolished
	July 14: Constitution accepted by the king
1791	June 20–25: Flight of the king
	September 30: National Constituent Assembly ends
	October 1: **Legislative** Assembly meets
1792	February 7: Austrian-Prussian alliance against **revolutionary** France
	August 10: Storming of the Tuileries
	September 2–6: The September massacres
	September 21: National Convention meets. Abolition of the **monarchy**
	December: Trial of Louis XVI before the National Convention
1793	January 21: Execution of Louis XVI
	February 1: War declared against Great Britain, Holland, and Spain
	March: **Royalist** revolt in the Vendée region of western France
	April: Committee of Public Safety gains real power
	October 16: Execution of Marie Antoinette, beginning of the Reign of Terror
	December: Retreat of the Allies across the Rhine
1794	April 5: Execution of Georges Danton and his allies
	July 27: Fall of Robespierre (the Ninth Thermidor)
1795	April 1: Bread riots in Paris
	August 22: Constitution of 1795
	October 5: Napoleon crushes disturbance in Paris
	October 26: National Convention terminated
1796	May 10: Battle of Lodi (Napoleon in Italy)
1797	October 17: Treaty of Campo Formio (Austria forced to recognize French gains in Italy)
1798	April: Helvetic Republic proclaimed in Switzerland
	July 21: Battle of the Pyramids (Napoleon defeats Turks in Egypt)
1799	August 24: Napoleon leaves Egypt
	November 9: The "18 Brumaire" overthrow of the Directory
	December 24: Constitution of the Year VIII guarantees Napoleon almost unlimited powers as First Consul
1802	March 27: Peace of Amiens ends European fighting for fourteen months
1804	Napoleon crowns himself Emperor of France
1805	October 21: Napoleon's fleet defeated by Great Britain's Royal Navy under the command of Lord Nelson at the Battle of Trafalgar
1805–6	French victories at Austerlitz (1805) and Jena (1806) drive Austria, Prussia, and Russia out of European wars

Sources for Further Research

Plain, Nancy. *Louis XVI, Marie Antoinette and the French Revolution.* Tarrytown,
    N.Y.: Marshall Cavendish Corporation, 2001.

Shuter, Jane, Ed. *Helen Williams and the French Revolution.* New York: Raintree
    Publishers, 1996.

Stewart, Ross. *The French Revolution.* Chicago: Raintree Publishers, 2003.

List of Primary Sources

The author and publisher gratefully acknowledge the following sources from which
written excerpts in the book are drawn. In some cases, the wording or sentence
structure has been simplified to make the material appropriate for a school readership.

P.9   Marie Antoinette: www.fordham.edu/halsall/mod/1773marieantoinette.html
P.11 Articles from the cahiers: history.hanover.edu/texts/cahiers3.html
P.13 Arthur Young: *The Faber Book of Reportage*: John Carey, Ed. Faber & Faber, 1987.
P.15 Emmanuel-Joseph Sieyès: http://www.fordham.edu/halsall/mod/sieyes.html
P.17 Louis XVI: chnm.gmu.edu/revolution/d/303/
P.19 Louis de Flue: chnm.gmu.edu/revolution/d/383/
P.21 Jean-Sylvain Bailly: www.woodberry.org/acad/hist/FRWEB/ MARCH/documents/bailly.htm
P.23 Declaration of the Rights of Man: www.hrcr.org/docs/frenchdec.html
P.25 Decree of the National Constituent Assembly: www.historyteacher.net/APEuroCourse/Readings
        Open/ Reading-FrRevol-AbolitionOfNobility-1790.htm
P.27 King's Declaration: www.woodberry.org/acad/hist/FRWEB/ FLIGHT/documents/kingword.htm -
P.29 "La Marseillaise": www.geocities.com/revolutioninfrance/culture.html
P.31 The Times: *The Faber Book of Reportage*: John Carey, Ed. Faber & Faber, 1987.
P.33 Henry Essex Edgeworth: *The Faber Book of Reportage*: John Carey, Ed. Faber & Faber, 1987.
P.35 Georges Danton: *ThePenguin Book of Historic Speeches:* 1995. Brian MacArthur, Ed. 1995.
P.37 J.G. Millingen: *The Faber Book of Reportage*: John Carey, Ed. Faber & Faber, 1987.
P.39 Maximilien Robespierre: *The Faber Book of Reportage*: John Carey, Ed. Faber & Faber, 1987.
P.41 Pierre-Toussaint Durand de Maillane: chnm.gmu.edu/revolution/d/441/
P.43 Celestin Guillard de Floriban: *Journal de Celestin Guillard de Floriban, bourgeois de Paris sous la
        Revolution.* R. Aubert, Ed. 1974. Reprinted in *The Oxford History of the French Revolution*:
        William Doyle, Oxford University Press, 1989.
P.45 Napoleon: chnm.gmu.edu/revolution/d/461/
P.47 Napoleon: chnm.gmu.edu/revolution/d/518/
P.49 Victor Hugo: chnm.gmu.edu/revolution/d/587/
P.51 Alexis de Tocqueville: chnm.gmu.edu/revolution/d/590

Glossary

aristocrat   noble person who usually has wealth and a high social position

assassin   someone hired to kill someone else

bayonet   blade on the end of a rifle

besieger   part of a force that is trying to capture a fortress or other protected position

bias   judgement that is influenced by personal opinion

black market   illegal sale of restricted goods, often at high prices

blockade   surrounding or blocking a place by an enemy to prevent entry and exit of supplies

censorship   controlling what can be said in public or written

clergy   priests, bishops, and other religious people

colonist   someone who has left her or his native land to settle in a territory controlled by the home country

confinement   prevented from leaving a place, usually by soldiers or other security forces

conscript   someone who has been forced into military service

conservative   opposed to political change, or a person who holds that view

conspirator   person who is linked with a secret plot

constitution   written statement of a country's government outlining the rights and liberties of its people

contemporaries   those who lived at the time

contradiction   statement that seems to disagree with accepted facts

counterrevolutionaries   people who try to overthrow a revolutionary government and return a country to the old system

dauphin   eldest son of a king of France

deliberating   discussing and arguing over before reaching a decision

democracy   system of government that tries to represent all the people in a country fairly by giving as many people as possible the chance to vote

despotic   governing with little or no concern for public opinion

detriment   worsening

dictator   leader who has total control, with no restrictions

dissolve   (of a political group) to stop a session or meeting

Enlightenment   period in the 17th and 18th centuries when writers and artists sought to bring happiness and justice to the world

executive   related to carrying out laws

exile   being forced to live away from one's own country, often because of political beliefs against the government

feudal   system of land ownership in which a single rich land owner controls the lives of those who work on the land

fraternity   quality of being brotherly

guillotine   machine for beheading people that has a large blade that slides down a channel onto a block

hereditary   inherited at birth

Holy Roman Empire   a Germanic empire in central Europe that lasted from 800 B.C.E. until 1806

legislative   having the power to create laws

legislature   branch of a government in which representatives discuss and pass laws

liberal   favoring change in society, or a person who holds that view

moderate   not extreme

monarchy   government or a system of government where a country is ruled by a king or royal family

oppression   harsh behavior by a government or ruler against the people

orator   public speaker

pamphlets   booklets written and distributed to support a political cause

pestilence   harmful disease

pike   weapon with a long wooden handle and a pointed metal head

pillage   to rob violently

primary source   original document describing a historical event or era

propaganda   information that is meant to sway or change public opinion

provisional   temporary

radical   favoring extreme change in society, or a person who favors that

republic   system of government in which leaders are elected or chosen rather than hereditary

republicans   people favoring a republican style of government

revolution   dramatic change (often in government) that replaces an old way of life with something new

revolutionary   person or group favoring, working toward such a change

rostrum   stand for public speaking

royalist   person who supports monarchy

scaffold   raised wooden platform used for the execution of criminals

secondary source   historical record that is written by someone who was not present when an event took place

treason   crime of betraying one's country to a foreign (often enemy) power

tribunal   special court for trying political cases

tyranny   rule by brute power

tyrant   cruel or oppressive leader

unanimous   with everyone agreeing

undemocratic   system where leaders are not elected

universal suffrage   system of voting in which every adult (or, in the 18th century, every adult male) has the right to vote

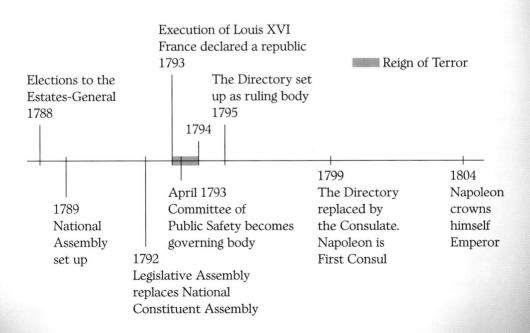

Execution of Louis XVI
France declared a republic
1793

Reign of Terror

Elections to the
Estates-General
1788

The Directory set
up as ruling body
1795

1794

1789
National
Assembly
set up

April 1793
Committee of
Public Safety becomes
governing body

1792
Legislative Assembly
replaces National
Constituent Assembly

1799
The Directory
replaced by
the Consulate.
Napoleon is
First Consul

1804
Napoleon
crowns
himself
Emperor

Index